AMY ELLIS

Modern Basics

Easy Quilts to Fit Your Budget, Space, and Style

Modern Basics:
Easy Quilts to Fit Your Budget, Space, and Style
© 2011 by Amy Ellis

That Patchwork Place® is an imprint of
Martingale & Company®.

Martingale & Company
19021 120th Ave. NE, Suite 102
Bothell, WA 98011 USA
www.martingale-pub.com

Mission Statement

Dedicated to providing
quality products and service
to inspire creativity.

Credits

President & CEO: Tom Wierzbicki
Editor in Chief: Mary V. Green
Managing Editor: Tina Cook
Developmental Editor: Karen Costello Soltys
Technical Editor: Ursula Reikes
Copy Editor: Marcy Heffernan
Design Director: Stan Green
Production Manager: Regina Girard
Illustrator & Designer: Adrienne Smitke
Photographer: Brent Kane

Special thanks to
Vicki and Matt Howe of Redmond, Washington, and
Karen and Jim Clifton of Monroe, Washington, for
generously allowing us to photograph in their homes.

Printed in China
16 15 14 13 12 11   8 7 6 5 4 3

**Library of Congress Cataloging-in-Publication Data
is available upon request.**

ISBN: 978-1-60468-015-7

Contents

Introduction

I often encounter people who "don't have time to quilt," and I think to myself that they may be more in need of a creative outlet than anyone! As a mom with four young children (2, 4, 6, and 9 as I'm writing this), I know that having the time to quilt can be a challenge, but so rewarding too. For me, quilting is my creative therapy in the midst of our busy household. Taking time for myself to create, is relaxing and fulfilling.

In these pages you'll find simple, interesting quilts that can be broken down into manageable projects, no matter how little time you have. I've learned a quilt doesn't have to be complicated to be beautiful or well loved by its recipient. I encourage you to cut the pieces for the entire quilt and keep each block at the same point of production. This is how I work daily, and I continue to see progress in my projects without losing motivation or pieces.

If you're lacking space for a quilting area in your home, set up shop on your kitchen or dining table—that's what I've done! Make room for fabric under your bed or in a spare dresser drawer. I typically don't buy fabric just for my stash—there isn't space in our home. By making purchases for a specific project, I ensure that the fabrics will be used and our home won't be overflowing with fabric. Purchase or repurpose a small plastic tote or sewing basket for tools and notions as they accumulate and find a spot to quickly stow your sewing machine when it's mealtime. You probably have more space than you realize!

I hope you enjoy the pages in front of you and the quilts you create.

—Amy

Designed and pieced by Amy Ellis; machine quilted by Natalia Bonner

Basic Ease

FINISHED QUILT: 60½" X 72½" ❋ FINISHED BLOCK: 12" X 12"

This quilt is simple yet interesting, and it's a great project to ease you into quilting. Find beautiful fabrics and sew this quilt, learning as you go!

Materials

Yardages are based on 42"-wide fabrics.

1⅝ yards of cream with blue dot print for blocks
1⅝ yards of medium blue floral for blocks
1⅜ yards of dark blue floral for blocks
⅝ yard of pink-and-red print for binding
4½ yards of fabric for backing
66" x 78" piece of batting

Enjoy the Process

I've learned that perfection is overrated! No one is perfect, plus the little imperfections give a quilt more character and serve as a reminder to its recipient that it was made with love. Enjoying the process is far more important to me than making it flawless! Each new quilt gives me another chance to learn and grow as a quilter. More than anything, I hope that you enjoy the process!

Cutting

From the cream with blue dot print, cut:
8 strips, 6½" x 42"

From the medium blue floral, cut:
8 strips, 6½" x 42"

From the dark blue floral, cut:
10 strips, 4½" x 42"; crosscut into 30 rectangles, 4½" x 12½"

From the pink-and-red print, cut:
7 binding strips, 2½" x 42"

Piecing the Blocks

1. Pin and sew a cream with blue dot strip to a medium blue floral strip. Press the seam allowances toward the medium blue floral. Make eight strip sets.

Make 8 strip sets.

2. Cut the strip sets into 30 segments, 8½" wide.

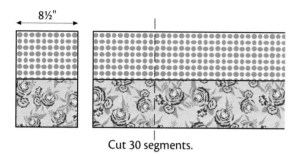

8½"

Cut 30 segments.

3. Pin and sew a dark blue floral rectangle to the right side of a segment from step 2. Press the seam allowances toward the dark blue floral rectangle. Repeat to make 30 blocks.

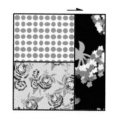

Make 30 blocks.

4. Trim and square the blocks to 12½" x 12½".

Assembling the Quilt Top

1. Lay out six rows of five blocks each, orienting the blocks as shown. Pin and sew the blocks together in rows, pressing the seam allowances in alternate directions from row to row.

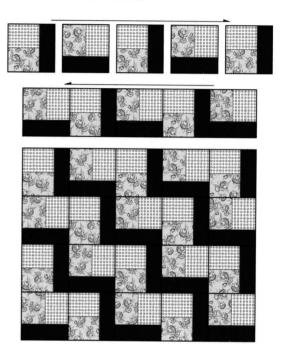

2. Pin and sew the rows together to complete the quilt top. Press the seam allowances in one direction.

Finishing the Quilt

1. Cut the length of the backing fabric in half to create two 80"-long pieces. Sew the two pieces together side by side and press the seam allowances open.

2. Referring to "Basting a Quilt Sandwich" on page 59, layer the backing, batting, and quilt top; then baste the layers together. Use your favorite quilting technique to quilt a design that you love.

3. Referring to "Binding" on page 60 and using the pink-and-red 2½"-wide strips, bind your quilt.

Tumbling Cubes

FINISHED QUILT: 60½" X 60½" ❊ FINISHED BLOCK: 12" X 12"

A quilt made of solid fabrics can be very appealing. Prints work too; try playing with the scale of prints for an equally exciting quilt. The color combinations are limitless; have fun finding the best colors for your quilt.

Materials

Yardages are based on 42"-wide fabrics.

4½ yards of medium gray solid for blocks and binding
¼ yard of teal solid for blocks
¼ yard of red solid for blocks
3¾ yards of fabric for backing
66" x 66" piece of batting

Cutting

There are a lot of pieces in this quilt block, but don't let that intimidate you! I love to cut systematically to keep track of the pieces, and chain piecing (page 58) helps the blocks come together quickly.

From the medium gray solid, cut:
9 strips, 4½" x 42"; crosscut into 25 rectangles,
    4½" x 12½" for piece I
34 strips, 2½" x 42"; crosscut into:
    50 rectangles, 2½" x 12½", for pieces G and H
    25 rectangles, 2½" x 9½", for piece E
    25 rectangles, 2½" x 8½", for piece F
    25 squares, 2½" x 2½", for piece D
    25 rectangles, 2½" x 1½", for piece C
6 binding strips, 2½" x 42"

From the teal solid, cut:
2 strips, 2½" x 42; crosscut into 25 squares,
    2½" x 2½", for piece B

From the red solid, cut:
2 strips, 2½" x 42; crosscut into 25 squares,
    2½" x 2½", for piece A

Piecing the Blocks

1. Arrange pieces A through H in the block formation to keep all the pieces in order.

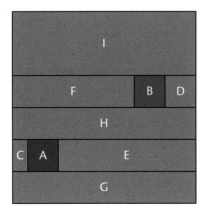

Designed and pieced by Amy Ellis; machine quilted by Natalia Bonner

2. Pin and sew piece C to piece A, and piece B to piece D. Press the seam allowances as shown. Make 25 units of each.

Make 25.   Make 25.

3. Pin and sew piece F to the B/D unit, and piece E to the C/A unit. Press the seam allowances as shown. Make 25 units of each.

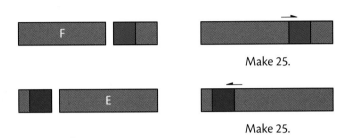

Make 25.

Make 25.

4. Pin and sew piece I to the F/B/D unit. Press the seam allowances toward piece I. Make 25 units.

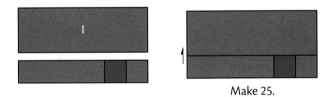

Make 25.

5. Pin and sew pieces G and H to the opposite sides of the C/A/E unit. Press the seam allowances toward pieces G and H. Make 25 units.

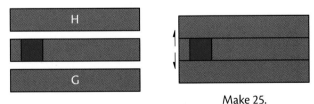

Make 25.

6. Pin and sew both halves of the block together. Press the seam allowances toward piece H. Make 25 blocks.

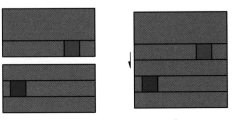

Make 25.

7. Trim and square the blocks to 12½" x 12½".

Assembling the Quilt Top

1. Lay out five rows of five blocks each, orienting the blocks as shown. Pin and sew the blocks together in rows, pressing the seam allowances in alternate directions from row to row.

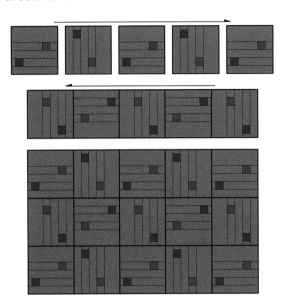

2. Pin and sew the rows together to complete the quilt top. Press the seam allowances in one direction.

Finishing the Quilt

1. Cut the length of the backing fabric in half to create two 67"-long pieces. Sew the two pieces together side by side and press the seam allowances open.

2. Referring to "Basting a Quilt Sandwich" on page 59, layer the backing, batting, and quilt top; then baste the layers together. This quilt is a blank slate for quilting. I asked quilter Natalia Bonner to use random straight lines to complement the modernity of the design. Use your favorite quilting technique to quilt a design that makes you happy!

3. Referring to "Binding" on page 60 and using the gray 2½"-wide strips, bind your quilt. Enjoy!

Designed and pieced by Amy Ellis; machine quilted by Natalia Bonner

1, 2, 3!

FINISHED QUILT: 72½" X 96½" ❋ **FINISHED BLOCK: 12" X 12"**

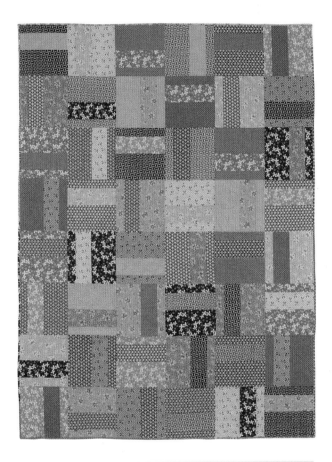

This quilt goes together in a snap. Instructions are given for a twin-size quilt; see optional fabric requirements for a baby quilt and a lap quilt.

Materials

All yardages are based on 42"-wide fabric unless otherwise noted.

½ yard *each* of 16 assorted prints for blocks

¾ yard of fabric for binding (I used leftover strips cut from prints for the blocks.)

5¾ yards of fabric for backing

78" x 102" piece of batting

Optional Quilt Sizes

Baby Quilt

For a baby quilt, piece 12 blocks to make a 36½" x 48½" quilt. You'll need:

½ yard *each* of 4 assorted prints for blocks

½ yard of fabric for binding

1½ yards of fabric for backing

42" x 54" piece of batting

Lap Quilt

For a lap quilt, piece 30 blocks for a 60½" x 72½" quilt. You'll need:

½ yard *each* of 10 assorted prints for blocks

⅝ yard of fabric for binding

4 yards of fabric for backing

66" x 78" piece of batting

Cutting

From *each* of the 16 assorted prints, cut:

1 strip 6½" x 42"; crosscut into 3 rectangles, 6½" x 12½" (48 total), for piece C

1 strip 4½" x 42"; crosscut into 3 rectangles, 4½" x 12½" (48 total), for piece B

1 strip 2½" x 42"; crosscut into 3 rectangles, 2½" x 12½" (48 total), for piece A

From the binding fabric, cut:

9 strips, 2½" x 42"

Piecing the Blocks

Mix up your prints for a fantastic scrappy look in your quilt. I like to sit on the couch with my pins and take my time deciding which combination I like best for each block.

1. Pin and sew piece A to piece B. Press the seam allowances toward piece B. Make 48 units.

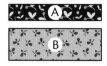 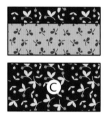

Make 48.

2. Pin and sew piece C (matching piece A) to the bottom of the A/B unit. Press the seam allowances toward piece C. Make 48 blocks.

Make 48.

3. Trim and square the blocks to 12½" x 12½".

Assembling the Quilt Top

1. Lay out eight rows of six blocks each, orienting the blocks as shown. Take your time balancing the colors within the quilt top. Pin and sew the blocks together in rows, pressing the seam allowances in alternate directions from row to row.

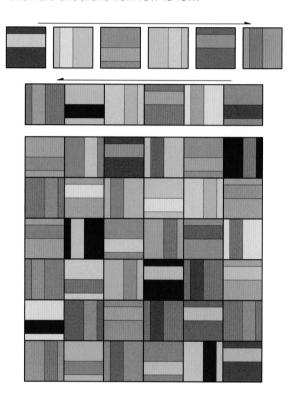

2. Pin and sew the rows together to complete the quilt top. Press the seam allowances in one direction.

Finishing the Quilt

1. Cut the length of the backing fabric in half to create two 103"-long pieces. Sew the two pieces together side by side and press the seam allowances open.
2. Referring to "Basting a Quilt Sandwich" on page 59, layer the backing, batting, and quilt top; then baste the layers together. Use your favorite quilting technique to quilt.
3. Referring to "Binding" on page 60 and using the 2½"-wide strips, bind your quilt.

Modern V

FINISHED QUILT: 48½" X 72½" ❈ FINISHED BLOCK: 12" X 12"

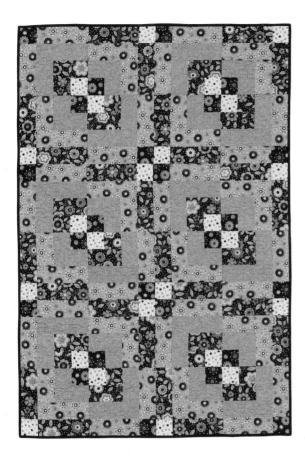

Alternating blocks create a fun pattern within this quilt. Color placement is the key to this simple block. Look for saturated colors in your fabric choices for the best contrast.

Materials

Yardages are based on 42"-wide fabrics.

1 ¼ yards of green print for blocks
1 ⅛ yards of teal print for blocks
1 ⅛ yards of large-scale brown print for blocks
⅜ yard of medium-scale brown print for blocks
⅜ yard of cream print for blocks
⅝ yard of brown print for binding
4 ½ yards of fabric for backing
54" x 78" piece of batting

Cutting

From the green print, cut:
11 strips, 3½" x 42"; crosscut into:
    36 rectangles, 3½" x 9½", for pieces F,
        G, and M
    12 rectangles, 3½" x 6½", for piece L

From the teal print, cut:
8 strips, 3½" x 42"; crosscut into:
    24 rectangles, 3½" x 6½", for pieces D and K
    12 rectangles, 3½" x 9½", for piece E
    12 squares, 3½" x 3½", for piece J

From the large-scale brown print, cut:
9 strips, 3½" x 42"; crosscut into:
    12 squares, 3½" x 3½", for piece B
    12 rectangles, 3½" x 6½", for piece C
    24 rectangles, 3½" x 9½", for pieces N and O

From the medium-scale brown print, cut:
3 strips, 3½" x 42"; crosscut into 24 squares,
    3½" x 3½", for pieces H and I

From the cream print, cut:
3 strips, 3½" x 42"; crosscut into 24 squares,
    3½" x 3½", for pieces A and P

From the brown print, cut:
7 binding strips, 2½" x 42"

Designed and pieced by Amy Ellis; machine quilted by Natalia Bonner

Piecing the Blocks

1. Arrange the cut pieces in the block formation for block 1 and block 2 to keep all the pieces in order.

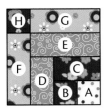
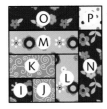

Block 1   Block 2

2. Pin and sew piece A to piece B, and piece I to piece J. Press the seam allowances as shown. Make 12 of each.

Make 12.

Make 12.

3. Pin and sew piece C to the A/B unit, and piece K to the I/J unit. Press the seam allowances as shown. Make 12 of each.

Make 12.

Make 12.

4. Pin and sew piece D to the A/B/C unit, and piece L to the I/J/K unit. Press the seam allowances as shown. Make 12 of each.

Make 12.

Make 12.

5. Pin and sew piece E to the A/B/C/D unit, and piece M to the I/J/K/L unit. Press the seam allowances as shown. Make 12 of each.

Make 12.

Make 12.

6. Pin and sew piece F to the A/B/C/D/E unit, and piece N to the I/J/K/L/M unit. Press the seam allowances as shown. Make 12 of each.

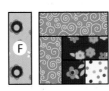

Make 12.

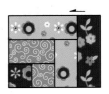

Make 12.

7. Pin and sew piece G to piece H, and piece O to piece P. Press the seam allowances as shown. Make 12 of each.

Make 12.

Make 12.

8. Pin and sew unit G/H to the A/B/C/D/E/F unit, and unit O/P to the I/J/K/L/M/N unit. Press seam allowances as shown. Make 12 each of block 1 and block 2.

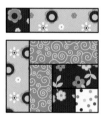
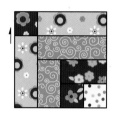

Block 1.
Make 12.

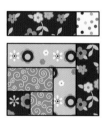
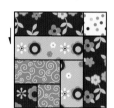

Block 2.
Make 12.

9. Trim and square the blocks to 12½" x 12½".

Assembling the Quilt Top

1. Lay out six rows of four blocks each, alternating block 1 and block 2 and orienting them as shown. Pin and sew the blocks together in rows, pressing the seam allowances in alternate directions from row to row.

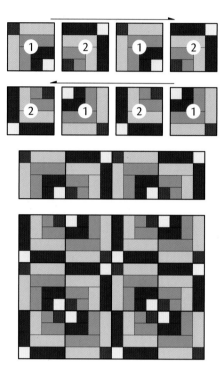

2. Pin and sew the rows together to complete the quilt top. Press the seam allowances in one direction.

Finishing the Quilt

1. Cut the length of the backing fabric in half to create two 80"-long pieces. Sew the two pieces together side by side and press the seam allowances open.
2. Referring to "Basting a Quilt Sandwich" on page 59, layer the backing, batting, and quilt top; then baste the layers together. Use your favorite quilting technique to quilt.
3. Referring to "Binding" on page 60 and using the brown print 2½"-wide strips, bind your quilt.

Posie Patch

FINISHED QUILT: 54½" X 54½" ❈ FINISHED BLOCK: 9" X 9"

This is a fast and easy quilt made with a Layer Cake (precut fabric bundle; see page 55), and it includes an introduction to appliqué. With these few instructions, you'll be ready to personalize all your quilts.

Materials

Yardages are based on 42"-wide fabrics.

1 Layer Cake of your choice OR ⅜ yard *each* of 10 different fabrics cut into 40 squares, 10" x 10", for blocks, appliqué flowers, and flower centers
⅛ yard of olive print for appliqué stems
½ yard of blue print for binding
3½ yards of fabric for backing
60" x 60" piece of batting
Steam-A-Seam for appliqué

Cutting

From the olive print, cut:
1 strip, 1½" x 42"
1 strip, 1" x 42"

From the blue print, cut:
6 binding strips, 2½" x 42"

> ### One Block at a Time
> I encourage you to make decisions one block at a time. Look for contrast in each pair, and it will work out in the end. Laying out all the pieces at this point may be overwhelming and very time consuming.

Piecing the Blocks

1. Cut each of 36 squares in half diagonally to make 72 triangles.

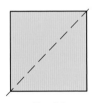

Cut 36.   Make 72 triangles.

2. Select pairs of triangles contrasting in color and pattern. Pin along the diagonal and sew. This diagonal line, or bias, has a lot of stretch; be careful not to pull your block out of square as you sew and press. Press the seam allowances open. Make 36 blocks. While pressing toward the dark fabric is the most common practice for a quilter, when I'm working with triangles, I prefer to press my seam allowances open. Pressing this way makes

Designed and pieced by Amy Ellis; machine quilted by Natalia Bonner

matching seams easier later and reduces bulk within the quilt top.

Press seam allowances open. Make 36.

3. Trim and square the blocks to 9½" x 9½".

Assembling the Quilt Top

1. Lay out six rows of six blocks each, orienting the diagonal seams as shown. Look for movement in the color and print arrangement. Move the blocks around on your design wall or floor until you feel confident that you love the layout. Pin and sew the blocks together in rows, pressing the seam allowances in alternate directions from row to row.

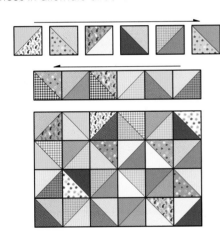

Design Wall

If you have wall space available, a large piece of flannel tacked on a wall is helpful for arranging blocks. However, if you don't have wall space, the floor works too. If you're having trouble deciding on a layout, taking a picture and viewing it on your computer helps to see where the trouble spots are.

2. Sew the rows together to complete the quilt top. Press the seam allowances in one direction.

Adding the Appliqué

No need to pull out the needle and thread to attach appliqués. Steam-A-Seam is an appliqué product that makes it simple. Follow the manufacturer instructions for use.

1. For the circle shapes, I traced dishes in my kitchen. My large circles measure 8", 7", and 6½" in diameter and the small inner circles measure 3½", 2¾", and 2½" in diameter. Search your cupboards for bowls and cups that fit on your Steam-A-Seam and are proportional for your flowers.

2. To make the flower stems, cut the 1"- and the 1½"-wide olive print strips in half crosswise; then trim them to length after you have decided on placement. Cut strips of Steam-A-Seam the same width and length as the fabric strips for the flower stems.

3. Refer to the photograph on page 20 or play with the arrangement of the appliqué pieces to find the placement that you like. Pin the pieces in place before transferring the quilt to the ironing board.

4. Using a damp pressing cloth, slowly steam all the pieces in place. A pressing cloth is usually a dish towel in my house; look for one without texture. The pressing cloth protects your iron from any extra sticky residue on the edges and ensures a well-adhered appliqué. Start at the top with the flowers and work your way down the stem to alleviate any puckers or unwanted excess.

5. Once you have all of your pieces in place, you may stitch around them with a zigzag stitch, blanket stitch, or even a straight stitch. Or you may decide to quilt over the top like Natalia did on my quilt. It's up to you!

Finishing the Quilt

1. Cut the length of the backing fabric in half to create two 63"-long pieces. Sew the two pieces together side by side and press the seam allowances open.

2. Referring to "Basting a Quilt Sandwich" on page 59, layer the backing, batting, and quilt top; then baste the layers together. Use your favorite quilting technique to quilt a design that you love.

3. Referring to "Binding" on page 60 and using the 2½"-wide blue strips, bind your quilt.

Designed and pieced by Amy Ellis; machine quilted by Natalia Bonner

Wind Power

FINISHED QUILT: 72½" X 72½" ❉ FINISHED BLOCK: 12" X 12"

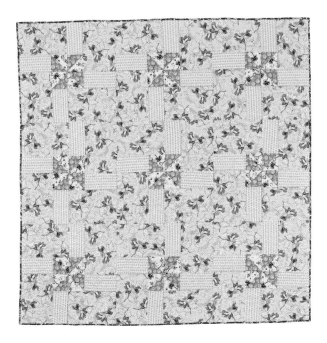

This quilt introduces a traditional method for making half-square triangles. Once this method is mastered, the options for quilt designs are many!

Materials

Yardages are based on 42"-wide fabrics.

3¼ yards of aqua print for blocks
1⅓ yards of pink print for blocks
½ yard of white print for blocks
½ yard of teal print for blocks
⅔ yard of fuchsia print for binding
4½ yards of fabric for backing
78" x 78" piece of batting

Baby Quilt Option

For a baby quilt, make 16 blocks for a quilt measuring 48½" x 48½". You'll need:

1⅝ yards of aqua print
⅝ yard of pink print
¼ yard *each* of white and teal prints
½ yard of fabric for binding
3 yards of fabric for backing
54" x 54" piece of batting

Cutting

From the aqua print, cut:
12 strips, 8½" x 42"; crosscut into 36 rectangles, 8½" x 12½"

From the pink print, cut:
9 strips, 4½" x 42"; crosscut into 36 rectangles, 4½" x 8½"

From the white print, cut:
3 strips, 5" x 42"; crosscut into 18 squares, 5" x 5"

From the teal print, cut:
3 strips, 5" x 42"; crosscut into 18 squares, 5" x 5"

From the fuchsia print, cut:
8 binding strips, 2½" x 42"

Piecing the Blocks

1. Mark a diagonal line on the wrong side of the 18 white 5" squares.

Mark 18 squares.

2. Pin a white square on top of a teal square. Sew ¼" away from both sides of the drawn line. Repeat with the rest of the pairs of white and teal squares.

Sew 18 pairs.

3. Cut along the marked diagonal line, to create two half-square-triangle units. Press the seam allowances open. Make 36 half-square-triangle units.

**Cut to make 36
half-square-triangle units.**

4. Trim the half-square-triangle units to 4½" x 4½". Be sure to align the diagonal line on the ruler with the diagonal seam. Depending on your ¼" seam allowance, you may or may not need to trim much off.

5. Lay out the cut fabrics and half-square-triangle units in the block formation to keep all the pieces in order. Pin and sew a pink rectangle to a half-square-triangle unit. Press the seam allowances toward the pink rectangle. Make 36 units.

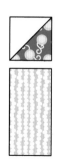 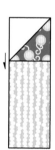

Make 36.

6. Pin and sew an aqua rectangle to the unit from step 5. Press the seam allowances toward the aqua rectangle. Make 36 blocks.

Make 36.

7. Trim and square the blocks to 12½" x 12½".

Assembling the Quilt Top

1. Lay out six rows of six blocks each, orienting the blocks as shown. Pin and sew the blocks together in rows, taking care to match the seams in your pinwheels. Press the seam allowances in alternate directions from row to row.

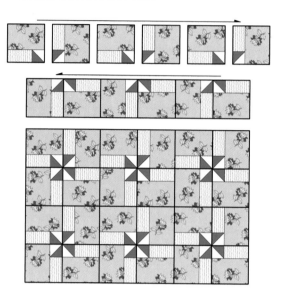

2. Pin and sew the rows together to complete the quilt top. Press the seam allowances in one direction.

Finishing the Quilt

1. Cut the length of the backing fabric in half to create two 80"-long pieces. Sew the two pieces together side by side and press the seam allowances open.

2. Referring to "Basting a Quilt Sandwich" on page 59, layer the backing, batting, and quilt top; then baste the layers together. Use your favorite quilting technique to quilt a design you love.

3. Referring to "Binding" on page 60 and using the fucshia 2½"-wide strips, bind your quilt.

Graduation

FINISHED QUILT: 58½" X 58½"

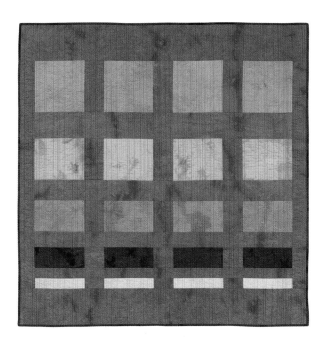

This bold geometric quilt is made without constructing blocks; just cut and sew your top together!

Materials

Yardages are based on 42"-wide fabrics.

2½ yards of sienna solid fabric for sashing and border
⅞ yard of brown solid for body and binding
⅔ yard of blue solid
⅜ yard of gold solid
⅜ yard of green solid
¼ yard of cream solid
3½ yards of fabric for backing
64" x 64" piece of batting

Cutting

From the blue solid, cut:
2 strips, 10½" x 42"; crosscut into 4 squares, 10½" x 10½"

From the gold solid, cut:
2 strips, 8½" x 42"; crosscut into 4 rectangles, 8½" x 10½"

From the green solid, cut:
2 strips, 6½" x 42"; crosscut into 4 rectangles, 6½" x 10½"

From the brown solid, cut:
2 strips, 4½" x 42"; crosscut into 4 rectangles, 4½" x 10½"
6 binding strips, 2½" x 42"

From the cream solid, cut:
2 strips, 2½" x 42"; crosscut into 4 rectangles, 2½" x 10½"

From the sienna solid, cut the following strips crosswise first:
4 strips, 4½" x 42"; crosscut into:
   3 rectangles, 4½" x 10½"
   3 rectangles, 4½" x 8½"
   3 rectangles, 4½" x 6½"
   3 rectangles, 4½" x 4½"
   3 rectangles, 4½" x 2½"

From the sienna solid, cut the following strips *lengthwise*:
1 strip, 5½" x 52½"
1 strip, 4½" x 52½"
1 strip, 3½" x 52½"
1 strip, 2½" x 52½"
2 strips, 3½" x 44½"
2 strips, 7½" x 58½"

Designed and pieced by Amy Ellis; machine quilted by Natalia Bonner

Organizing Your Pieces

I've found binder clips from the office-supply store to be a nice way to keep pieces together without having pins out for little fingers to find. You could also slip a piece of paper in there for labeling pieces.

Assembling the Quilt Top

1. Pin and sew a sienna sashing rectangle to the appropriate-sized colored rectangle. Repeat for each of the remaining colored rectangles. Press the seam allowances as shown. Make three of each color.

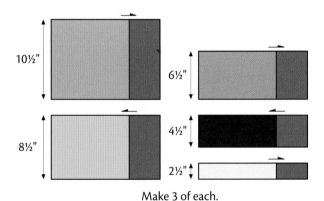

Make 3 of each.

2. Lay out three matching units from step 1 and a matching colored rectangle at the right end. Pin and sew the units together to make one row of blocks for each color. Press the seam allowances as shown.

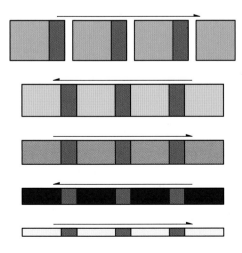

3. You're ready to add the horizontal sashing strips. Pin and sew the blue 10½"-wide row to a 5½" x 52½" sashing strip. Press the seam allowances toward the sashing strip.

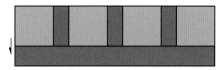

4. Pin and sew the gold 8½"-wide row to a 4½" x 52½" sashing strip. Press the seam allowances toward the sashing strip.

5. Pin and sew the green 6½"-wide row to the 3½" x 52½" sashing strip. Press the seam allowances toward the sashing strip.

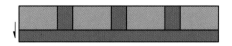

6. Pin and sew the brown 4½"-wide row to the 2½" x 52½" sashing strip. Press the seam allowances toward the sashing strip.

7. Pin the cream 2½"-wide row to the bottom of the assembled row from step 6. To line up the seams, slide a long ruler between the layers, lay the edge of the ruler along the seam of one row of blocks, and line up the corresponding seam on the other row of blocks. Remove the ruler without moving the fabric, and pin in place. Sew the rows together.

8. Lay out the rows and sashing strips as shown. Pin and sew them together, making sure to line up the seams. Press the seam allowances toward the sashing strips.

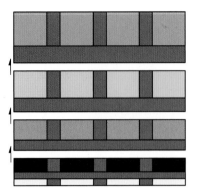

9. Pin and sew the 3½" x 44½" borders to the sides. Press the seam allowances toward the borders, and trim any excess. Pin and sew the 7½" x 58½" borders to the top and bottom. Press the seam allowances toward the borders, and trim any excess.

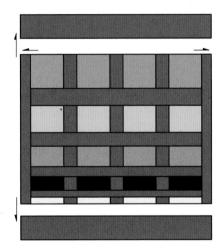

Finishing the Quilt

1. Cut the length of the backing fabric in half to create two 63"-long pieces. Sew the two pieces together side by side and press the seam allowances open.
2. Referring to "Basting a Quilt Sandwich" on page 59, layer the backing, batting, and quilt top; then baste the layers together. This quilt is very minimalistic, and straight lines of quilting add to the design. You don't even have to measure; add a line of quilting here and there and see what you think.
3. Referring to "Binding" on page 60 and using the brown 2½"-wide strips, bind your quilt.

FINISHED QUILT: 60" X 84" ❋ FINISHED BLOCK: 12" X 12"

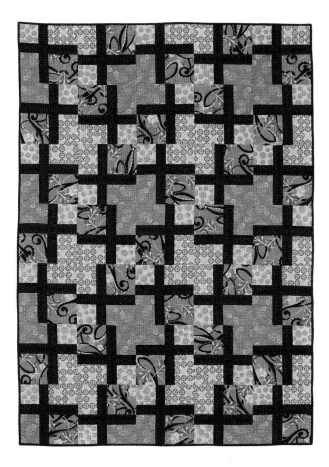

This quilt is a fun way to show off some of your favorite fabrics —each has a turn being the star of your quilt!

Materials

Yardages are based on 42"-wide fabrics.

2⅜ yards of brown print for blocks and binding
1¼ yards of pink print for blocks
1⅛ yards of green print for blocks
⅞ yard of cream print for blocks
¾ yard of cream with green dot print for blocks
5 yards of fabric for backing
66" x 90" piece of batting

Cutting

From the brown print, cut:
31 strips, 2½" x 42"; crosscut 12 of the strips
    into 35 rectangles, 2½" x 12½"

From the pink print, cut:
6 strips, 6½" x 42"

From the green print, cut:
5 strips, 6½" x 42"

From the cream print, cut:
6 strips, 4½" x 42"

From the cream with green dot print, cut:
5 strips, 4½" x 42"

Piecing the Blocks

1. Pin and sew a cream with green dot strip, a brown strip, and a green strip together. Press the seam allowances toward the brown strips. Make five strip sets.

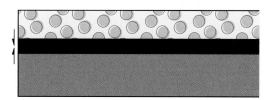

Make 5 strip sets.

2. From the strip sets made in step 1, cut 35 segments, 4½" wide.

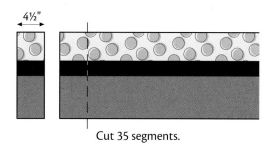

Cut 35 segments.

Designed and pieced by Amy Ellis; machine quilted by Natalia Bonner

3. Pin and sew a cream print strip, a brown strip, and a pink strip together. Press the seam allowances toward the brown strip. Make six strip sets.

Make 6 strip sets.

4. From the strip sets made in step 3, cut 35 segments, 6½" wide.

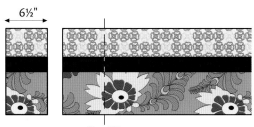

Cut 35 segments.

5. Pin and sew a 4½"-wide segment from step 2, a brown rectangle, and a 6½"-wide segment from step 4 together as shown. Press the seam allowances toward the brown rectangle. Make 35 blocks.

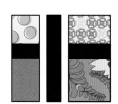 

Make 35.

6. Trim and square the blocks to 12½" x 12½".

Assembling the Quilt Top

1. Lay out seven rows of five blocks each, orienting the blocks as shown. Pin and sew the blocks together in rows, pressing the seam allowances in alternate directions from row to row.

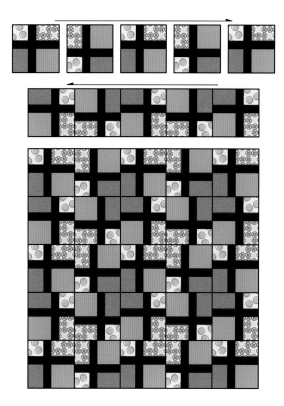

2. Sew the rows together to complete the quilt top. Press the seam allowances in one direction.

Finishing the Quilt

1. Cut the length of the backing fabric in half to create two 90"-long pieces. Sew the two pieces together side by side and press the seam allowances open.
2. Referring to "Basting a Quilt Sandwich" on page 59, layer the backing, batting, and quilt top; then baste the layers together. Use your favorite quilting technique to quilt.
3. Referring to "Binding" on page 60 and using the remaining brown 2½"-wide strips, bind your quilt.

Designed and pieced by Amy Ellis; quilted by Natalia Bonner

Basic Puzzle

FINISHED QUILT: 50½" X 60½"

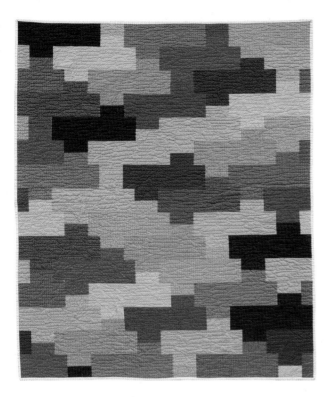

This quilt is made without blocks; instead there are three different rows that repeat in a variety of colors. I've listed my colors, or you may select your own! A gradation of color in one color family would be beautiful, as would a fall-inspired palette. There are so many options!

Materials

Yardages are based on 42"-wide fabrics.

⅓ yard each of 12 assorted solids*
½ yard of white solid for binding
3¾ yards of fabric for backing
56" x 66" piece of batting

I used Kaufman Kona Cotton in the following colors: aloe, asparagus, azure, glacier, hibiscus, lapis, leaf, medium gray, palm, periwinkle, plum, and pomegranate.

Optional Large Quilt

For a larger quilt, 68" x 96", you'll need:

⅝ yard each of 12 assorted colors. Cut 8 large rectangles and 16 small rectangles from each color and lay out 24 rows of 4 rectangles.
⅝ yard of fabric for binding
5¾ yards of fabric for backing
74" x 102" piece of batting

Cutting

From each of the 12 solids, cut:
2 strips, 4½" x 42"; crosscut into:
    4 rectangles, 4½" x 14½" (48 total)
    8 rectangles, 2½" x 4½" (96 total)

From the white solid, cut:
6 binding strips, 2½" x 42"

Assembling the Quilt Top

With no blocks to assemble, this quilt top can be sewn up without delay! As this quilt is a bit of a puzzle, I suggest using a design wall to arrange the pieces for the quilt. I started by laying out all my large rectangles randomly for steps 1, 2, and 3 below until I found a pleasing arrangement of colors. Follow the directions for adding small rectangles and for piecing the first three rows to make all the rows in the quilt.

1. For the first row, arrange three large rectangles and four small rectangles as shown. Pin and sew the pairs of small rectangles together on the long sides and sew them between the large rectangles. Press the seam allowances open.

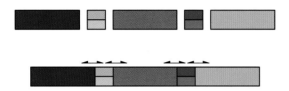

2. For the second row, select three large rectangles and six small rectangles, matching the rectangles to the row above and below as shown. Cut the far-right rectangle into two pieces measuring 4½" x 8½" and 2½" x 4½". Arrange the pieces as shown. Pin and sew the small rectangles together first; then sew the row together. Press the seam allowances open.

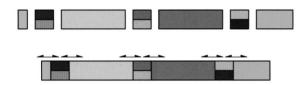

3. For the third row, select three large rectangles and six small rectangles, matching the rectangles to the row above and below as shown. Cut the far-left rectangle into two pieces measuring 4½" x 8½" and 2½" x 4½". Arrange the pieces as shown. Pin and sew the small rectangles together first; then sew the row together. Press the seam allowances open.

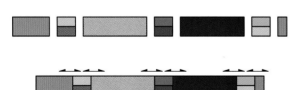

4. Sew the first, second, and third rows together. Press the seam allowances open.

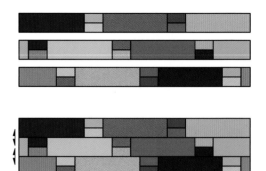

5. Repeat steps 1 through 4 another four times to make the remaining 12 rows and sew all the rows together. Be sure to match large and small rectangles to the colors in previous rows. Press the seam allowances open.

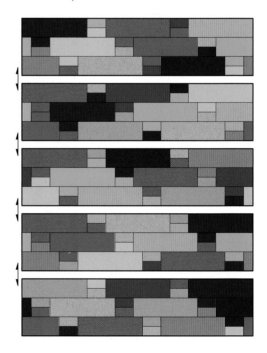

Finishing the Quilt

1. Cut the length of the backing fabric in half to create two 67"-long pieces. Sew the two pieces together side by side and press the seam allowances open.

2. Referring to "Basting a Quilt Sandwich" on page 59, layer the backing, batting, and quilt top; then baste the layers together. Use your favorite quilting technique to quilt a design that you love.

3. Referring to "Binding" on page 60 and using the white 2½"-wide strips, bind your quilt.

Modern Cabin

FINISHED QUILT: 72½" X 72½" ❋ FINISHED BLOCK: 12" X 12"

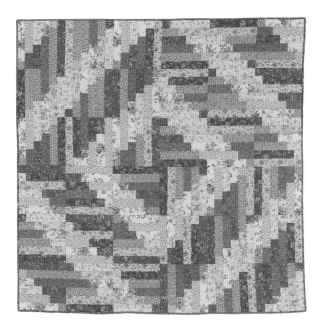

Strip piecing gives this classic block a remake with the same eye-catching appeal. There are many ways to orient your blocks, too! You may want to experiment with the layout before sewing your quilt top together.

Materials

Yardages are based on 42"-wide fabrics.

4¼ yards *total* of assorted blue prints for blocks
3 yards *total* of assorted cream prints for blocks
⅔ yard of blue print for binding
4½ yards of fabric for backing
78" x 78" piece of batting

Baby Quilt Option

For a baby quilt measuring 48½" x 48½", you'll need:

1½ yards total of assorted blue prints for blocks
1 yard total of assorted cream prints for blocks
½ yard of blue print for binding
3 yards of fabric for backing
54" x 54" piece of batting

Instead of 3 strip sets, you'll just need 1 for each of the required units.

Cutting

From the assorted blue prints, cut:
15 strips, 2½" x 42"; crosscut 12 of the strips into 36 rectangles, 2½" x 12½"
3 strips, 4½" x 42"
3 strips, 6½" x 42"
3 strips, 8½" x 42"
3 strips, 10½" x 42"

From the assorted cream prints, cut:
3 strips, 2½" x 42"
3 strips, 4½" x 42"
3 strips, 6½" x 42"
3 strips, 8½" x 42"
3 strips, 10½" x 42"

From the blue print, cut:
8 binding strips, 2½" x 42"

Designed and pieced by Amy Ellis; machine quilted by Natalia Bonner

Piecing the Blocks

1. Pin and sew a cream 10½"-wide strip to a blue 2½"-wide strip. Press the seam allowances toward the blue fabric. Make three of strip-set A.

Make 3 of strip set A.

2. Pin and sew a cream 8½"-wide strip to a blue 4½"-wide strip. Press the seam allowances toward the blue fabric. Make three of strip-set B.

Make 3 of strip set B.

3. Pin and sew a cream 6½"-wide strip to a blue 6½"-wide strip. Press the seam allowances toward the blue fabric. Make three of strip-set C.

Make 3 of strip set C.

4. Pin and sew a cream 4½"-wide strip to a blue 8½"-wide strip. Press the seam allowances toward the blue fabric. Make three of strip-set D.

Make 3 of strip set D.

5. Pin and sew a cream 2½"-wide strip to a blue 10½"-wide strip. Press the seam allowances toward the blue fabric. Make three of strip-set E.

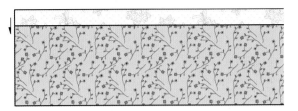

Make 3 of strip set E.

6. From each of strip-sets A, B, C, D, and E, cut 36 segments 2½" wide (180 segments total).

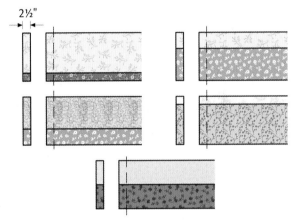

Cut 36 segments from each of the strip sets (total 180 segments).

7. Lay out the cut segments in the block formation to keep all the pieces in order. Pin and sew one each of segments A, B, C, D, E, and a blue rectangle together as shown. Press the seam allowances open. Make 36 blocks.

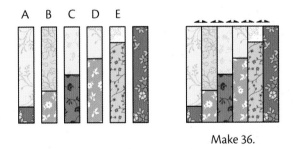

Make 36.

8. Trim and square the blocks to 12½" x 12½".

Assembling the Quilt Top

1. Lay out six rows of six blocks each, orienting the blocks as shown. Pin and sew the blocks together in rows, pressing the seam allowances in alternate directions from row to row.
2. Pin and sew the rows together to complete the quilt top. Press the seam allowances in one direction.

Finishing the Quilt

1. Cut the length of the backing fabric in half to create two 80"-long pieces. Sew the two pieces together side by side and press the seam allowance open.
2. Referring to "Basting a Quilt Sandwich" on page 59, layer the backing, batting, and quilt top; then baste the layers together. Use your favorite quilting technique to quilt.
3. Referring to "Binding" on page 60 and using the blue print 2½"-wide strips, bind your quilt.

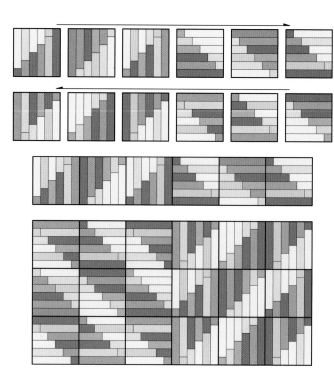

Twisted Bars

FINISHED QUILT: 66" X 78" ❄ FINISHED BLOCK: 12" X 12"

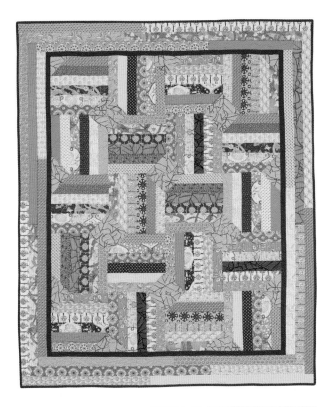

This quilt can be made using precut fabrics, or with scraps from various projects. The corner triangles unite the blocks, and the borders continue the scrappy theme.

Materials

Yardages are based on 42"-wide fabrics.

2 Jelly Rolls (precut fabric bundle; see page 55) OR
    5 yards of assorted prints, cut into 66 strips,
    2½" x 42", for pieced outer border and blocks
1 yard of brown solid for inner border and binding
¾ yard of aqua print for blocks
4½ yards of fabric for backing
72" x 84" piece of batting

Cutting

From the aqua print, cut:
5 strips 4½" x 42"; crosscut into 40 squares,
    4½" x 4½"

From the brown solid, cut:
8 strips 1½" x 42"
8 binding strips 2½" x 42"

Piecing the Blocks

1. Pin and sew six assorted 2½"-wide strips together. Press the seam allowances all in one direction. Make seven strip sets.

Make 7 strip sets.

2. Measure the width of the pressed strip sets. They should measure 12½"; if not, it's okay, make note of the width and use it to cut your squares. Cut 20 squares, 12½" x 12½", or the measurement of your strip sets.

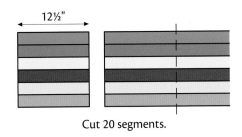

Cut 20 segments.

3. Draw a diagonal line on the wrong side of the aqua 4½" squares.

Mark 40 squares.

39

Designed and pieced by Amy Ellis; machine quilted by Natalia Bonner

4. Pin two squares to opposite corners of a 12½" square as shown. Sew *on* the drawn diagonal line. Repeat on the remaining squares.

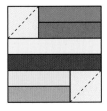

Make 20.

5. Trim ¼" away from the diagonal seam sewn in step 4. Press the seam allowances open.

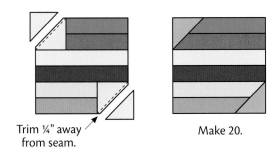

Trim ¼" away from seam.

Make 20.

6. Trim and square the blocks to 12½" x 12½".

Assembling the Quilt Top

1. Lay out five rows of four blocks each, orienting the blocks as shown or in another arrangement that pleases you. Pin and sew the blocks together in rows, pressing the seam allowances in alternate directions from row to row.

2. Pin and sew the rows together to complete the quilt top. Press the seam allowances in one direction.

3. Sew pairs of brown, 1½"-wide strips together end to end for the inner border. Pin and sew the brown 1½"-wide strips to the sides, and then the top and bottom, measuring and trimming the strips to fit. Press the seam allowances toward the brown strips. Sew the remaining assorted 2½"-wide strips together in pairs end to end to make long strips for borders. Add three more borders one at a time to the quilt top, measuring and trimming the strips to fit. Stagger the seams as you add borders to the sides, and then the top and bottom. Press the seam allowances toward the newly added border each time you add a border.

Finishing the Quilt

1. Cut the length of the backing fabric in half to create two 80"-long pieces. Sew the two pieces together side by side and press the seam allowance open.

2. Referring to "Basting a Quilt Sandwich" on page 59, layer the backing, batting, and quilt top; then baste the layers together. Use your favorite quilting technique to quilt.

3. Referring to "Binding" on page 60 and using the brown 2½"-wide strips, bind your quilt.

Designed and pieced by Amy Ellis; quilted by Natalia Bonner

Knotted Squares

FINISHED QUILT: 72½" X 72½" ❉ FINISHED BLOCK: 12" x 12"

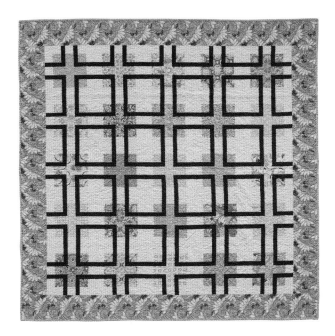

This bold and geometric quilt makes you stop and stare. Careful piecing yields fabulous results!

Materials

Yardages are based on 42"-wide fabrics.

2¼ yards of green print for borders

2 yards of white solid for blocks

1 Jelly Roll (precut fabric bundle; see page 55) OR
1¾ yards *total* of assorted prints cut into 25 strips, 2½" x 42"

1⅓ yards of brown solid for blocks

⅝ yard of coral print for binding, or use remaining strips from Jelly Roll

4½ yards of fabric for backing

78" x 78" piece of batting

Cutting

If using a Jelly Roll, select 25 of the strips to use in the blocks.

From *each* of the 25 Jelly Roll strips or 25 assorted strips, cut:
1 rectangle, 2½" x 10½" (25 total)
2 rectangles, 2½" x 3½" (50 total)
1 rectangle, 2½" x 8½" (25 total)

From the white solid, cut:
27 strips, 2½" x 42"; crosscut into:
   25 rectangles, 2½" x 10½"
   100 squares, 2½" x 2½"
   100 rectangles, 2½" x 4½"

From the brown solid, cut:
28 strips, 1½" x 42"; crosscut into:
   100 rectangles, 1½" x 4½"
   100 rectangles, 1½" x 5½"

From the green print, cut *lengthwise*:
2 strips, 6½" x 60½"
2 strips, 6½" x 72½"

From the coral print, cut:
8 binding strips, 2½" x 42"

Piecing the Blocks

I decided to press the seam allowances open in this block. This makes matching seams and sewing rows together during assembly much easier.

1. Pin and sew a white 2½" x 10½" strip to a print 2½" x 10½" strip along the long side. Press the seam allowances open. Make 25 strip sets.

Make 25 strip sets.

2. Cut each strip set made in step 1 into four segments, 2½" x 4½", for a total of 100 segments.

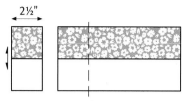

2½"

Cut 4 segments from each strip set.

3. Pin and sew a white 2½" x 4½" rectangle to each unit from step 2 as shown. Press the seam allowances open.

Make 100.

4. Pin and sew a brown 1½" x 4½" rectangle to each unit from step 3 as shown. Press the seam allowances open.

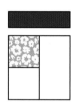

Make 100.

5. Pin and sew a brown 1½" x 5½" rectangle to each unit from step 4 as shown. Press the seam allowances open. Trim to 5½" square if necessary.

Make 100.

6. Pin and sew a white 2½" square to one end of a print 2½" x 3½" rectangle as shown. Press the seam allowances open. Make 50 units.

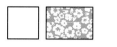

Make 50.

7. Pin and sew a white 2½" square to each end of each print 2½" x 8½" rectangle as shown. Press the seam allowances open.

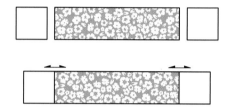

Make 25.

8. Pin and sew a unit from step 6 between two matching units from step 5, rotating the units as shown. Press the seam allowances open. Make 50 units.

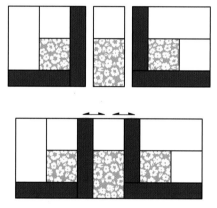

Make 50.

9. Pin and sew a unit from step 7 between two matching units from step 8 to make a block as shown. Press the seam allowances open. Make 25 blocks.

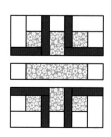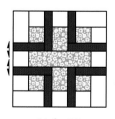

Make 25.

10. Trim and square the blocks to 12½" x 12½".

Assembling the Quilt Top

1. Lay out five rows of five blocks each referring to the quilt layout diagram below. Pin and sew the blocks together in rows, pressing the seam allowances open.

2. Pin and sew the rows together to complete the quilt top. Press the seam allowances in one direction.

Adding Borders

Pin and sew the green print 6½" x 60½" strips to the sides of the quilt top. Press the seam allowances toward the borders. Pin and sew the green print 6½" x 72½" strips to the top and bottom of the quilt top. Press the seam allowances toward the borders.

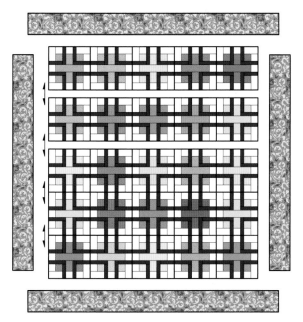

Quilt layout

Finishing the Quilt

1. Cut the length of the backing fabric in half to create two 81"-long pieces. Sew the two pieces together side by side and press the seam allowances open.

2. Referring to "Basting a Quilt Sandwich" on page 59, layer the backing, batting, and quilt top; then baste the layers together. Use your favorite quilting technique to quilt a design that you love.

3. Referring to "Binding" on page 60 and using the coral print 2½"-wide strips, bind your quilt.

Designed and pieced by Amy Ellis; machine quilted by Natalia Bonner

Basic Postage

FINISHED QUILT: 69" X 69" ❄ FINISHED BLOCK: 12" X 12"

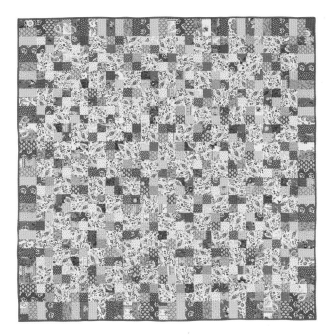

Traditional postage-stamp quilts are made with tiny 1" squares. I've enlarged the squares a little and added alternating larger squares to ease the process. This makes it a less-intimidating project for any quilter!

Materials

Yardages are based on 42"-wide fabrics.

1 Jelly Roll (precut fabric bundle; see page 55) OR
    3 yards *total* of assorted prints cut into 42 strips,
    2½" x 42", for blocks and borders
2 yards of white floral for blocks
½ yard of blue print for blocks and borders
⅝ yard of red print for binding
4¼ yards of fabric for backing
75" x 75" piece of backing

Cutting

From the white floral, cut:

14 strips, 4½" x 42; crosscut into 112 squares,
    4½" x 4½"

From the blue print, cut:

6 strips, 2½" x 42"

From the red print, cut:

7 binding strips, 2½" x 42"

Piecing the Blocks

Work the blue strips you cut into your Jelly Roll mix. Use 30 of the 46 strips to make strip sets, and set aside 16 strips for the borders.

1. Pin and sew a light and a dark 2½"-wide strip together. Make 15 strip sets. Press the seam allowances open to reduce bulk.

Make 15 strip sets.

2. Cut the strip sets into 226 segments, 2½" wide.

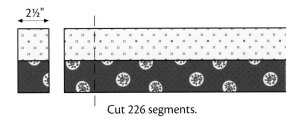

Cut 226 segments.

3. Pin, carefully matching the seams, and sew two segments together to make a four-patch unit. Press the seam allowances open. Repeat to make 113 four-patch units.

Make 113
four-patch units.

Easing Fabric as You Piece

Fabric is very forgiving. If your seams aren't matching up as you'd like, you may pull a little to ease the pieces together as you sew.

4. Pin and sew two four-patch units and one floral 4½" square together as shown. Press the seam allowances open. Make 38 of row A.

Row A.
Make 38.

5. Pin and sew two floral 4½" squares and one four-patch unit as shown. Press the seam allowances open. Make 37 of row B.

Row B.
Make 37.

6. Pin, carefully matching seams, and sew two row A and one row B together to make block 1. Press the seam allowances toward row B. Make 13 of block 1.

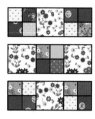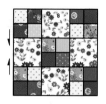

Block 1.
Make 13.

7. Pin, carefully matching seams, and sew two row B and one row A to make block 2. Press the seam allowances toward rows B. Make 12 of block 2.

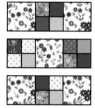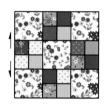

Block 2.
Make 12.

8. Trim and square the blocks to 12½" x 12½".

Assembling the Quilt Top

1. Lay out five rows of five blocks each, alternating block 1 and block 2 as shown. Pin and sew the blocks together in rows, pressing the seam allowances in alternate directions from row to row.

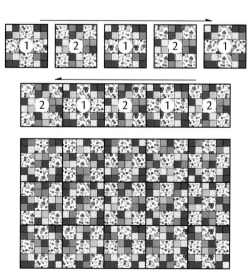

2. Pin and sew the rows together to complete the quilt top. Press the seam allowances in one direction.

Adding Borders

1. Sew four assorted 2½"-wide strips together to make a strip set. Press the seam allowances open. Make four strip sets. Cut each strip set into 8 segments, 4½" wide, for a total of 32 segments

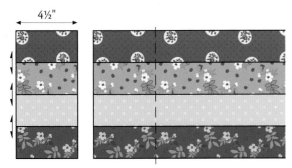

Make 4 strip sets.
Cut 8 segments from each (32 total).

2. Pin and sew 8 segments together to make a border. Press the seam allowances open. Make four borders.

3. Pin and sew one border to one side of the quilt top, stopping halfway. Press the seam allowances toward the border.

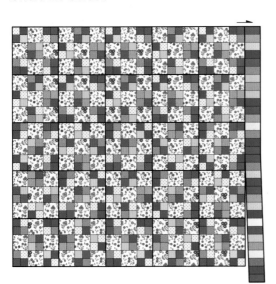

4. Working counterclockwise, pin and sew the remaining borders to the sides of the quilt top. Press seam allowances toward the borders. Finish sewing the first border to the quilt to complete the quilt top. Press the seam allowances toward the border.

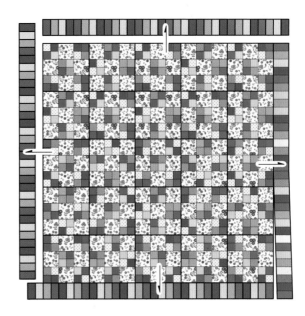

Finishing the Quilt

1. Cut the length of the backing fabric in half to create two 76"-long pieces. Sew the two pieces together side by side and press the seam allowances open.

2. Referring to "Basting a Quilt Sandwich" on page 59, layer the backing, batting, and quilt top; then baste the layers together. Use your favorite quilting technique to quilt.

3. Referring to "Binding" on page 60 and using the red 2½"-wide strips, bind your quilt.

Designed and pieced by Amy Ellis; machine quilted by Natalia Bonner

Modern Mirrors

FINISHED QUILT: 82½" X 90½" ❋ **FINISHED BLOCK: 10" X 14"**

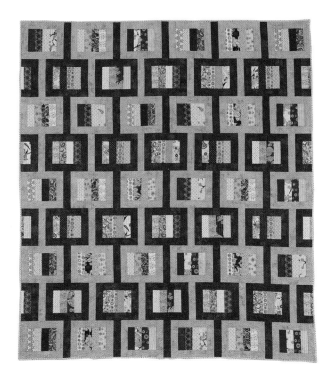

This striking quilt is beautiful and simple! I made it in a full size; however, it could easily be scaled down to suit your desired size.

Materials

Yardages are based on 42"-wide fabrics.

3¼ yards of aqua print for blocks

3 yards of brown solid for blocks

1 Jelly Roll (precut fabric bundle; see page 55) OR
    2⅞ yards *total* of assorted prints cut
    into 36 strips, 2½" x 42", for blocks

¾ yard of pink print for binding

6¾ yards of fabric for backing

88" x 96" piece of batting

Lap-Quilt Option

For a lap-sized quilt, make 28 blocks (16 aqua and 12 brown) for a 56" x 70" quilt. You'll need:

1 Jelly Roll for blocks

1⅞ yards of aqua print for blocks

1⅝ yards of brown solid for blocks

⅝ yard fabric or use remaining strips from Jelly
    Roll for binding

4½ yards of fabric for backing

62" x 76" piece of batting

Cutting

From the aqua print, cut:

36 strips, 2½" x 42"; crosscut 18 of the strips into:
    60 rectangles, 2½" x 8½"
    30 rectangles, 2½" x 10½"

From the brown solid fabric, cut:

30 strips, 2½" x 42"; crosscut 12 of the strips into:
    48 rectangles, 2½" x 8½"
    24 rectangles, 2½" x 10½"

From the pink print, cut:

9 binding strips, 2½" x 42"

Piecing the Blocks

1. Pin and sew together four assorted Jelly Roll strips to make a strip set. Press the seam allowances in one direction. Make nine strip sets.

Make 9 strip sets.

2. Cut the strip sets into 54 center segments, 6½" wide.

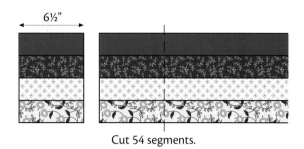

6½"

Cut 54 segments.

3. Pin and sew an aqua 2½" x 8½" rectangle to a center segment as shown. Pin and sew a brown 2½" x 8½" rectangle to a center segment as shown. Press the seam allowances toward the rectangles just added. Make 30 aqua units and 24 brown units.

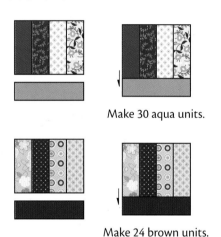

Make 30 aqua units.

Make 24 brown units.

4. Pin and sew an aqua 2½" x 8½" rectangle to the left side of an aqua unit, and a brown 2½" x 8½" rectangle to the left side of a brown unit. Press the seam allowances toward the rectangles just added. Make 30 aqua units and 24 brown units.

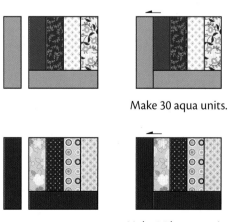

Make 30 aqua units.

Make 24 brown units.

5. Pin and sew an aqua 2½" x 10½" rectangle to the top of an aqua unit. Pin and sew a brown 2½" x 10½" rectangle to the top of a brown unit. Press the seam allowances toward the rectangles just added. Make 30 aqua units and 24 brown units.

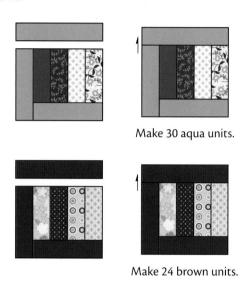

Make 30 aqua units.

Make 24 brown units.

6. Pin and sew an aqua 2½"-wide strip to a brown 2½"-wide strip to make a strip set. Press the seam allowances toward the brown fabric. Make 18 strip sets.

Make 18 strip sets.

7. Cut the strip sets from step 6 into 54 segments, 10½" wide.

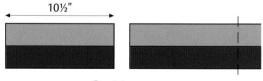

10½"

Cut 54 segments.

8. Pin and sew the 10½" segments from step 7 to the right-hand side of the units from step 5, placing the appropriate-colored strip next to the block to match the aqua or brown unit. Press the seam allowances toward the rectangles just added. Make 30 aqua blocks and 24 brown blocks.

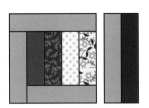 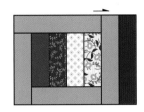

Make 30 aqua blocks.

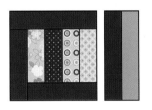 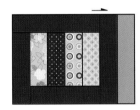

Make 24 brown blocks.

9. Trim the blocks to 10½" x 14½".

Assembling the Quilt Top

This top is a little challenging to put together, but the result is worth it! Make sure you have space to lay out your blocks.

1. Lay out six aqua blocks in a row. Pin and sew the blocks together. Press the seam allowances toward the right. Undo the stitching and remove the last brown strip at the right-hand end of the row. The row should measure 82½". Make five aqua rows.

Remove last
brown strip.

Make 5 aqua rows.

2. Cut four brown blocks between the second and third strips of the four Jelly Roll strips as shown; the right piece is one strip wider than the left piece.

3. Lay out the brown row as shown, with the half blocks placed on either end. Pin and sew the blocks together. Press the seam allowances toward the left. Cut 1" from each end of the row to compensate for the brown strip that was removed in step 1. The row should measure 82½". Repeat to make four brown rows.

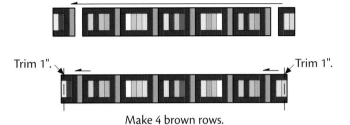

Trim 1".   Trim 1".

Make 4 brown rows.

4. Lay out the rows, alternating aqua and brown rows as shown. Pin and sew the rows together. Press the seam allowances in one direction.

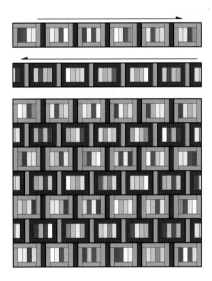

Finishing the Quilt

1. Cut the length of the backing fabric into three pieces; two 96"-long pieces and one 48"-long piece. Cut the 48"-long piece in half lengthwise and sew the pieces together end to end to make a third piece 96" long. Sew the three pieces together side by side and press the seam allowances open.

2. Referring to "Basting a Quilt Sandwich" on page 59, layer the backing, batting, and quilt top; then baste the layers together. Use your favorite quilting technique to quilt.

3. Referring to "Binding" on page 60 and using the pink print 2½"-wide strips, bind your quilt.

Quiltmaking Basics

The following pages include the basics for learning to make a quilt. They include lots of helpful tips if you're new to quilting or just need a refresher.

Tools

There is a wide range of tools and gadgets available for quilters. Honestly, I don't have many of them, because I have limited space available for my craft, and I like to keep things simple. I've included a list of the most basic necessities to make the quilts in this book.

Sewing machine: There are lots of fancy new machines, but the one you have in the closet from your mom or grandma works too! My first quilts were made with a ¾-size sewing machine with just nine stitch options. If you need to purchase a machine, don't break the bank—unless you're absolutely certain this will be a lifelong venture into quilting.

Rulers: Acrylic rulers make cutting precise and fast. There are countless rulers in different sizes and shapes, all very alluring. My favorite rulers are a 6½" x 24" for cutting strips and rectangles, a 6" square for cutting smaller pieces, and a 12½" square for trimming blocks after they've been sewn together. There are others that may be handy, but they're not necessary to make the quilts in this book.

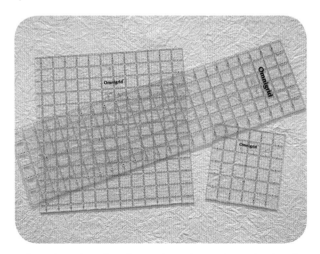

Three handy rulers for making the quilts in this book

Rotary cutter: The first tool to purchase for rotary cutting is the "pizza cutter" for fabric, which is super sharp and makes cutting precise pieces for your quilts easy. There are many types and sizes available. Find the one that is most comfortable for you.

Rotary-cutter options

Self-healing mat: This is the second tool to purchase for rotary cutting. Using this mat protects your surfaces and keeps your cutting blade in good shape. This is one tool that needs to be large in size; an 18" x 24" mat is a good size to allow you to cut the necessary strips.

Water-soluble pen: There are a variety of marking tools available for fabric. I tend to use an inexpensive option available at large fabric retailers. Any tool that you use needs to glide across the fabric smoothly so it doesn't pull the fabric as you mark it.

Sewing-machine needles: Needles come in lots of sizes. I use the general all-purpose 80/12 for piecing, and a slightly smaller 75/11 for machine quilting. If you ever actually hear your needle hitting the fabric, it's time to change your needle. It makes a "ping" sound when dull.

Thread: A general rule of thumb in quiltmaking is that the fabric content and thread content should be the same. So if using 100% cotton fabrics, use 100% cotton thread. This isn't always available, and colors may be limited, so use your discretion as needed.

Straight pins: I like to pin pieces together before sewing. My favorite pins are 1½" long with round, plastic heads. They're easy to hold onto when pinning.

Safety pins: Look for a large packet of safety pins available at fabric stores; they're used to baste the layers of the quilt together prior to quilting.

Hand-quilting thread: I like to use this stiffer, heartier thread for stitching my bindings in place. Having both warm and cool neutral colors around for just this purpose is very helpful.

Fabric

When selecting fabrics it's important to first and foremost LOVE the color and/or print. Personally, I have a hard time finishing a quilt if I don't love the fabrics I'm using. Keep this in mind as you browse fabric options. Once you've found one fabric that you love, find others that work with it. Balancing color, print, and value can take time for some to learn; others are blessed with a designer's eye. Step back and look at your fabric selections side by side to get a little perspective.

Also, consider adding solid fabrics to stretch your fabric budget. There is a large array of beautiful solid fabrics available, and a quilt made of solid fabrics only is a great lesson in working with value.

When possible, feel your fabric before purchasing. Is it soft? Is it thick? Is it thin? Is it stiff? Is it coarse? Most fabrics do soften up a little with washing, but they should be comfortable to your hand at the time you purchase them. If not, your quilt may not be as comfortable as you were hoping.

Buying Yardage

You can buy yardage, fat quarters (see right), or precut fabrics (see right) to make the quilts in this book. Or you can use a combination of any of the above. Treat all your fabrics in one quilt in the same manner.

Prior to cutting, always take the time to press your fabrics. I suggest using a spray starch for a nice crisp finish to the fabric, and I find that there is less stretching of the grain. I do not prewash my fabric, but you may if you like. When pressing, be careful not to distort the grain; instead of sliding the iron, lift and *press* as needed (see "Pressing" on page 58).

Buying Precut Fabrics

Precut fabrics are an excellent way to get a fast start on your quilting project! Precut fabrics should not be prewashed ever. They would end up a frayed and tangled mess in the wash.

Used in this book:

❋ Moda Jelly Roll—Forty 2½" x 42" to 44" strips
❋ Moda Layer Cake—Forty 10" x 10" squares

Also available:

❋ Moda Honey Bun—Forty 1½" x 42" to 44" strips
❋ Moda Turnover—Eighty 6" half-square triangles
❋ Charm pack—Forty-two 5" x 5" squares

Good to Know

Fat quarter: A quilting staple, this small cut of precious fabric measuring 18" x 22" offers more usable fabric than a traditional ¼-yard cut.

Selvage: This manufacturer-finished edge of the fabric typically includes identifiers for the fabric manufacturer. I've seen them saved and used in great selvage-only projects.

Length of fabric: This is the yardage that you purchased. Typically, strips are cut the width of the fabric, but occasionally borders are cut from the length of the fabric.

Width of fabric: This is the selvage-to-selvage width of the fabric. Most quilting cottons are 42" to 45" wide, while decorator fabrics are 54" to 60" wide.

Cutting

Always be careful using your rotary cutter—it's a round razor blade! Many quilters (me included) have scars on their fingers from when they got carried away and didn't look out for their fingers. Always keep your guard on the blade when it's not in use, and keep your fingers away from the edge of the ruler when cutting. Also, if you have young children or curious animals, take care to keep your rotary cutter out of their reach at all times.

Using a rotary cutter becomes easier with practice. Always apply firm pressure when cutting your fabric to ensure a straight cut through all the layers. Cut as many strips as possible with the width of your cutting mat; then adjust fabric.

Squaring the Edge of Your Fabric

Squaring your fabric is a necessary step prior to cutting strips; otherwise the strips will be cut on a slant. This may be a problem when cutting your smaller pieces; you may not be able to cut enough from the fabric allotted. Or when washed, your quilt may shrink oddly.

I square my fabric with each new length of fabric on the cutting mat. Verify that your fabric edge is square before cutting your next strip. Taking the time to learn this basic skill will prove very useful as you continue on your quilting journey.

1. Fold your fabric selvage to selvage.
2. Before laying your fabric down on your cutting mat, slide the selvages left or right until the fold of the fabric is flat. The cut edges of the fabric will most likely not be together.
3. Place the folded edge closest to you along a line on your cutting mat.
4. Align a second smaller ruler along the folded edge of the fabric. Place a long ruler to the left edge of the square, just covering the uneven raw edges of the fabric. Remove the smaller ruler and cut along the right-hand edge of the long ruler. Discard this strip.

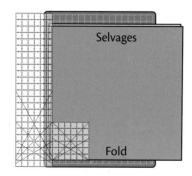

Cutting Strips and Segments

Cutting strips and then cutting segments from the strips is quick and easy. Verify the required width, and measure twice before cutting—you don't want to miscut your beautiful fabrics.

1. To cut strips, align the required measurement on the ruler with the newly cut edge of the fabric. For example, to cut a 2"-wide strip, place the 2" mark of the ruler on the edge of the fabric.

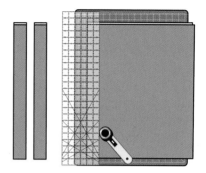

2. To cut squares and rectangles, cut strips in the required widths. With your ruler and rotary cutter, remove the selvage ends of the strip. Align the required measurements on the ruler with the left edge of the strip and cut a square or a rectangle. Continue cutting until you have the required number of pieces.

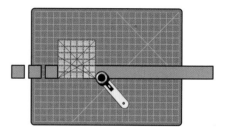

3. Cutting segments from strip sets is a speedy method used in a few of the quilts in this book. When cutting these segments, use the seam as your guide instead of the top or bottom edge. Often this means making the cut, and then rotating the segment to clean up the other edge as well. Don't worry about wasting fabric—extra fabric has been allowed in the materials.

   First, trim the ends of the strip set to square it up. Second, align the required measurement on the ruler with the left edge of the strip set, and align a horizontal line on the ruler with a seam in the strip set. Cut the required number of segments.

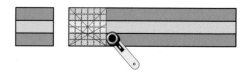

Piecing

I am not a perfectionist. I do aim for as close to perfection as possible, but I've learned that perfection comes at too high a price. The process of making a quilt is enjoyable if you allow yourself to enjoy it. If you do make a mistake, learn from it and move on. Don't point it out, and no one else will notice. And each quilt will be better than the last!

Getting an Accurate ¼" Seam Allowance

Perfecting your ¼" seam allowance will make quilting easier. If you have a ¼" foot with your sewing machine, great!

¼" foot for sewing machine

If you don't have a ¼" foot, do not dismay. Using tape or a permanent marker, mark ¼" away from your center needle position on your footplate. Take a few minutes to verify that you have an accurate ¼" seam allowance by following these steps:

1. Cut two 2½" squares.
2. Sew them together on one side. Press the seam allowances.
3. Measure your unit. It should measure 4½" exactly.

If your unit does not measure 4½", consider moving your needle to the right one or two positions or moving your tape slightly closer. If you move your needle, be certain that your presser foot can accommodate the shift, or you may break a needle. Work through the above steps to verify that you have perfected your ¼" seam allowance. If you're not able to perfect your ¼" seam allowance, don't give up. Being consistent is just as important. Your blocks may be slightly smaller, but the result will be just as beautiful.

Using Pins

I like to pin pieces together en masse and make a large stack of seams to sew. That way I'm certain that my edges are lined up and ready to sew without having to stop and double-check each one. This helps me to use my time efficiently when I'm able to sit and sew. See chain piecing on page 58.

Pinning your pieces in place before stitching is imperative to getting accurate points and matching seam junctions. When matching seams, I like to pin on either side of the seam, perpendicular to the seam being sewn.

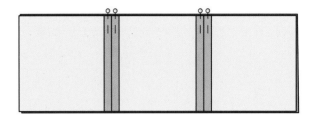

To pin, place the pieces right sides together; then slightly open the sides you plan to sew. Verify that your seams match, and then pin. Using one pin on either side is a good reminder for me to slow down and take the pin out just as I am about to sew over it. Word of caution: don't sew over your pins. You may break a needle, which can send the tip flying. Stay safe.

When joining rows, always match your seams first, then the beginning/end of the rows, and middle of the rows as needed. When matching seams and joining rows, there may be a touch of excess on one side. It happens—thankfully fabric is very forgiving. It's possible to ease the excess into the seam while pinning, by spreading the excess out as much as possible. Then work slowly over the seam while sewing. If after you have sewn, the seam is not matching as you'd like, take out the portion that's misaligned; then turn it over, repin, and sew from the other side. I've found I'm able to get it on the second try when I turn it over. When possible, placing the side with the excess on the bottom next to the feed dogs is most helpful as well.

Chain Piecing

When I have a stack of pinned pieces ready to sew, I like to piece them one after the other. This way I use less thread and I don't have to hold the threads to start my seam with each unit sewn. Chain piecing is a big time-saver.

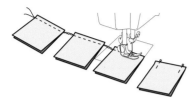

Pressing

Gentle pressing is also an imperative step in sewing a quilt top that lies flat. Pressing is different from ironing in that you lift the iron instead of pushing it over the fabric. In the projects, I've indicated which direction to press your seam allowances, and in some cases I've instructed you to press them open. I've found that pressing seam allowances open reduces bulk and helps the quilt to lie flat; both are a big plus when it's time to quilt. However you decide to press, setting your seams prior to pressing helps reduce stretching and movement in your seams. To set, press each seam just as you have sewn it.

Pressing to one side

Lay the sewn strip set on the ironing board, with the fabric you are pressing toward on top. Press the seam flat to set it. Use the edge of the iron to press the fabric over the seam. Be careful not to stretch the pieces out of shape as you press.

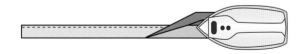

Pressing seam allowances open

1. Lay the sewn strip set on the ironing board. Press the seam flat to set it.
2. Open the sewn strip set and lay it right side down.
3. Run the iron along the seam, pressing it open with the tip of your iron.

4. Turn the strip set over to press it once more from the right side.

You don't have to purchase the most expensive iron to be a great quilter—if you don't have an iron, purchase a model that you can afford and use it until it quits. I've found the key to a lasting iron is removing the water from the steam tank at the end of each use. Storing water in the iron may cause it to rust, and then leak onto your projects.

Using Your Seam Ripper

When you eventually need to take out a seam or two (it happens to all of us), take a few moments to run your seam ripper under the stitches on the wrong side of your fabrics. Then turn over your piece and gently tug the thread loose.

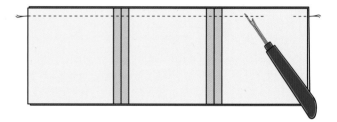

If you're removing a small segment from a long seam, you'll need to clip the thread on either end prior to resewing the seam. Hopefully you only need to resew once. Try three times at most, or you may ruin your fabric entirely.

Trimming Your Blocks

Most of the unfinished blocks in this book measure 12½". When you've finished piecing your blocks, take a few moments to trim. This is why I love my 12½" x 12½" ruler. Cutting all the edges flush will make things much simpler when you move on to sewing your quilt top.

Place the 12½" ruler on top of the block, centering the block by aligning the lines in the ruler with some of the seam lines in the block. Trim two edges of the block. Rotate the block and trim the other two edges.

Adding Borders

In the projects with borders, I've given you instructions for cutting borders to specific lengths. That's a good starting point; however, the best-fitting border is the one that you measure to fit your top.

1. Before adding your borders, lay out your quilt and measure the length of the quilt top through the middle. Cut two border strips to that measurement. Mark the center of the quilt edges and the border strips.

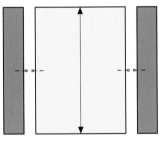

Measure center of
quilt, top to bottom.
Mark centers.

2. Pin the borders to the sides of the quilt top, matching the center marks and the ends and easing as necessary. Sew the borders in place and press the seam allowances as indicated in the instructions.

3. Measure the width of the quilt through the middle, including the side borders just added. Cut border strips to that measurement. Mark, pin, and sew the borders to the top and bottom as described for the side borders. Press the seam allowances as indicated in the instructions.

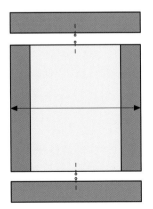 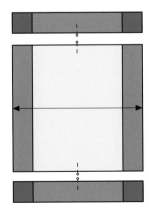

Measure center of
quilt, side to side.
Mark centers.

Basting a Quilt Sandwich

There are a few different ways to baste a quilt, but the most efficient (and budget friendly) is on the floor with safety pins. You can use the pins over and over, and they hold tight to the quilt, no matter how much you wrestle with your quilt getting it quilted.

Backing Measurements

I've given you instructions and provided adequate yardage for making your backing 6" larger than your quilt top, which means an extra 3" on all sides. This is plenty if you're going to be doing the quilting yourself. If you decide to have it quilted for you, check with the long-arm quilter to see how much larger she wants the backing. You may have to buy additional yardage for the backing.

1. Prepare your backing fabric, pressing out all the creases and wrinkles.
2. Lay your quilt back on the floor, right side down.
3. Use masking tape to tape the edges to the floor. Pull it tight, but don't stretch it, and avoid taping the corners. Taping the corners may cause the grain to be stretched out of square.
4. Lay the batting on top. Smooth out wrinkles with your hands or a cool iron for stubborn creases.
5. Add the quilt top, straighten, and smooth.
6. Using safety pins, begin pinning near the center and smooth out any excess fabric as you work your way out to the edges. Add a pin every 5" to 7" (or a hand length), until it's completely basted.

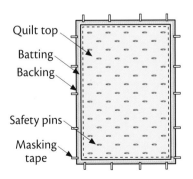

Quilt top
Batting
Backing

Safety pins
Masking
tape

Remove the tape and get ready to quilt!

Batting

There are a host of options for batting; experiment to see which one you like best. Cotton battings are more traditional and shift very little while quilting. While polyester battings are warmer, they also can be more challenging to quilt, due to the loft. These are things to keep in mind while selecting the right batting for your projects. Personally, I use Warm & Natural. I like the way it shrinks up when washed, and it's widely available.

Quilting Gloves

Quilting gloves are not a necessity, but they're really helpful if you're quilting on your domestic machine. They have grips on the fingers to help you move your fabric easily.

A darning or free-motion foot allows you to create any pattern you desire. Practice your desired pattern on paper to get a feel for how you need to move your fabric under the needle. When you're ready, put together a small quilt sandwich, about 18" square, and see how your machine responds. Before starting, shorten your stitch length to 0 and lower your feed dogs. This removes your machine's ability to feed the fabric and gives you complete control. From my own experience, this style of quilting is not learned overnight. Take time to practice and learn your machine's tension settings before taking the plunge to a quilt. That being said, not all machines have free-motion quilting capabilities, and your walking foot may be your best option. If your thread breaks constantly, or your tension is never equalized, you most likely will be more and more frustrated with the attempt to free-motion quilt.

When free-motion quilting, it's best to start quilting on one side and slowly work your way to the left or right, depending on what's most comfortable to you. Also, turning your machine perpendicular, so that the needle is closest to you offers more space to move the fabric under the needle. Try it and see how it feels to you.

After you've quilted your quilt, trim the batting and excess backing flush with your quilt top and make sure that it's square. Making sure that it's square often requires a little muscle; giving a little tug to your quilt prior to trimming is acceptable.

Machine Quilting

Quilting with your standard sewing machine is possible! Check your machine booklet for any instructions specific to your machine. Quilting can be a challenge, depending on the size of your quilt, but watching the texture work into the quilt is so rewarding.

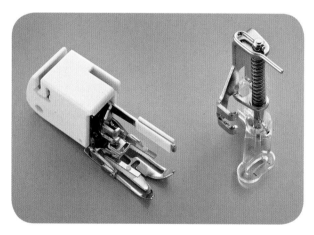

Walking foot and darning foot

If you haven't done any machine quilting yet, I recommend starting with your walking foot. The walking foot helps to feed the layers of your quilt evenly as you guide them under the needle. Obviously your walking foot will give you straight lines, but you can also give your quilt textured waves of quilting with a slight bit of movement. Other decorative stitches may be used too. Don't limit yourself or your machine.

Binding

When I was learning to quilt with books like this, the binding was the one piece of the quilt I could not visualize. I did it all sorts of ways, until it finally clicked for me. I hope that I explain it here so that you understand from the start.

Preparing the Binding

In all of the quilt projects you'll cut 2½"-wide strips for the binding and sew those strips together end to end at a 45° angle as follows:

1. With right sides together, lay one strip over the other at a 90° angle. Let the selvage end hang over the edge. Mark the diagonal, pin, and sew on the marked line. The first few times you do this, check that you have a straight strip of binding.

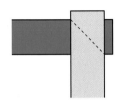

2. Trim away the excess, ¼" away from the seam, and press the seam allowances open.

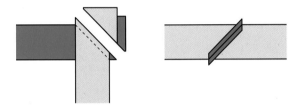

Repeat these steps until all of the strips are sewn together. Then press the entire length. Fold the binding in half with wrong sides together, and press. Your binding is now 1¼" wide, with a folded edge on one side and raw edges on the other. I like to fold my binding around a ruler while pressing to keep it nice and tidy, and then wear the binding strips as a bracelet while attaching it to my quilt top.

Attaching the Binding

I like to use my walking foot to attach the binding. Five layers of fabric and one layer of batting is a lot to keep track of, and the walking foot is a great tool.

If you feel the need to pin, you may, but I've found that if I take my time sewing the binding around the quilt, pinning isn't usually necessary.

1. On your quilt top, line up the raw edges of your quilt and the raw edges of your binding. Leave a tail of 10" to 12" and begin sewing in the middle of one side using a ¼" seam allowance. If you have a needle-down position on your sewing machine, it's helpful to put it down. That way when you stop sewing, the quilt will not shift out from under the needle as you maneuver the quilt and binding in place. When you arrive at a corner, stop sewing ¼" from the edge to add a fold to the corner. Remove your quilt from the sewing machine. Clip the thread.

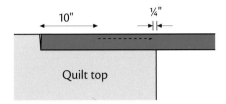

2. Turn the quilt so that you'll be stitching down the next side. Fold the binding up, away from the quilt. Then fold the binding back down onto itself, keeping the raw edges aligned with the edge of the quilt top. Begin stitching ¼" from the edge.

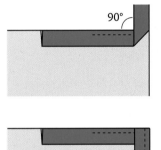

3. Continue around the quilt in the same manner until 18" away from where you began. Remove your quilt from the sewing machine to join the ends of the binding. Overlap the end of the binding on top of the beginning of the binding. Mark the end where it overlaps the beginning by 2½" and cut the excess.

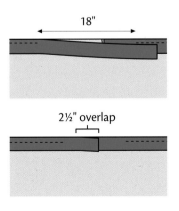

4. Unfold both sides of the bindings and lay them on top of each other at a 90° angle, with right sides together. Pin to keep the ends in place.

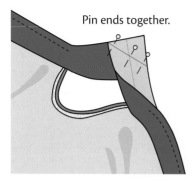

Pin ends together.

5. Mark a diagonal line as shown and sew on the line. Check to make sure the binding fits the edge of the quilt. Finish sewing the binding to the quilt.

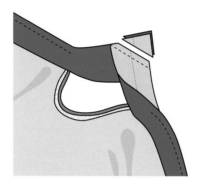

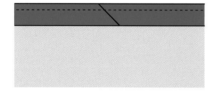

6. Press your binding away from the quilt top to ease the final step of turning the binding. One of my favorite ways to spend an evening is sitting on the couch tacking down a binding. Grab a needle, thimble, and hand-quilting thread to finish your quilt effortlessly. Blindstitch the binding in place with the folded edge covering the row of machine stitching. Start away from a corner and hide your knot in the raw edges. A miter will form at each corner. Blindstitch the miters in place.

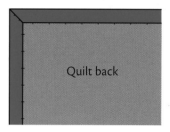

Quilt back

It's possible to bind a quilt entirely on the sewing machine. After sewing the binding to the quilt top, carefully press and pin your binding to the back. Sew the binding from the top of your quilt, paying careful attention to catch the binding on the back.

Quilt Community

A quick word on community—it's easy to get discouraged about your quilting when those around you aren't as enthusiastic about fabric and quilt blocks as you are. Consider visiting a quilt guild in your area, or look online for blogs about quilting. You'll be surprised by how much you can learn from both of these options.

ABOUT THE Author

Amy Ellis has been quilting for 10 years and sewing for 23. Having learned the basics of garment sewing as a girl, she caught the quilting bug with the birth of her first daughter. Today with four kids at home, quilting is her creative outlet, and she loves to inspire new quilters to find their own way.

Acknowledgments

Special thanks to:

My loving family: Joe, Ella, Emmalie, Sophia, and Owen. Your encouragement, enthusiasm, extra chores, and extra dinners have made this dream a reality. I love you all!

Natalia Bonner of Piece-N-Quilt for all the beautiful quilting! I couldn't have done it without you.

Art Gallery Fabrics, Moda Fabrics, Riley Blake Fabrics, and Windham Fabrics; each sent me beautiful fabrics to work with.

Blog readers who encourage and inspire me to continue dreaming and creating!

There's More Online!

You can see what Amy's been up to lately at amyscreativeside.com.

You might also enjoy these other fine titles from

Martingale & Company

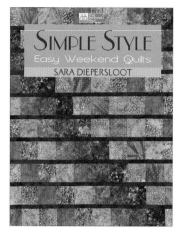

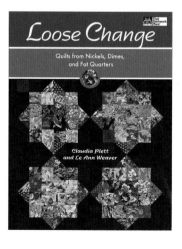

Our books are available at bookstores and your favorite craft, fabric, and yarn retailers.
Visit us at www.martingale-pub.com or contact us at:

1-800-426-3126
International: 1-425-483-3313
Fax: 1-425-486-7596
Email: info@martingale-pub.com

America's Best-Loved Craft & Hobby Books®
America's Best-Loved Knitting Books®

America's Best-Loved Quilt Books®